LIVING WELL

BICYCLE SAFETY

by Lucia Raatma

THE CHILD'S WORLD®
CHANHASSEN, MINNESOTA

The Child's World®

Published in the United States of America by The Child's World®
P.O. Box 326, Chanhassen, MN 55317-0326
800-599-READ
www.childsworld.com

Subject Consultant:
Bridget Clementi,
Safe Kids Coordinator,
Children's Health
Education Center,
Milwaukee, Wisconsin

Photo Credits: Cover: DiMaggio/Kalish/Corbis; Brand X Pictures/Picture Quest: 12 (Tyler Stableford), 19 (William McKellar); Corbis: 8 (Bob Rowan; Progressive Image), 11-right, 24 (Macduff Everton), 31 (Tom Stewart); Corbis/Picture Quest: 21, 26; elektraVision AG/Picture Quest: 13; Getty Images/Brand X Pictures: 25; James Leynse/Corbis Saba: 10; Kansas Department of Transportation: 9; Marc Romanelli/Brand X Pictures/Picture Quest: 22, 23; Myrleen Ferguson Cate/PhotoEdit: 5, 17; PhotoEdit: 6 (Tom Prettyman), 11 (Michael Newman); Photodisc/Picture Quest: 7 (Daisuke Morita), 14 (C. Sherburne/PhotoLink); Thinkstock/Picture Quest: 15, 16 (Ron Chapple), 18, 21-right.

The Child's World®: Mary Berendes, Publishing Director

Editorial Directions, Inc.: E. Russell Primm, Editorial Director; Elizabeth K. Martin and Katie Marsico, Line Editors; Olivia Nellums, Editorial Assistant; Susan Hindman, Copy Editor; Susan Ashley, Proofreader; Peter Garnham, Fact Checker; Tim Griffin/IndexServ, Indexer; Elizabeth K. Martin and Matthew Messbarger, Photo Researchers and Selectors

Library of Congress Cataloging-in-Publication Data
Raatma, Lucia.
  Bicycle safety / by Lucia Raatma.
     p. cm. — (Living well)
Includes index.
Summary: Explains the importance of being safe on a bicycle, whether alone or in a group, on the street or in a park, and points out specific things one can do to remain safe while cycling.
  ISBN 1-59296-085-5 (Library Bound : alk. paper)
  1. Bicycles—Safety measures—Juvenile literature. 2. Cycling—Safety measures—Juvenile literature. [1. Bicycles and bicycling—Safety measures. 2. Safety.] I. Title. II. Series: Living well (Child's World (Firm)
  GV1055.R32 2003
  796.6'028'9—dc21   2003006283

TABLE OF CONTENTS

CHAPTER ONE

KEISHA'S DAY OFF

Keisha could barely sit still to eat her breakfast. Today, she had a day off from school, and her mom had promised to take her on a bike ride. As soon as she finished eating, Keisha went outside to get her bike. She checked to be sure her brakes were working properly. Then she looked at her wheels to see if they needed any air.

"Okay, Mom, I'm ready," she called from the sidewalk.

"Oh no you're not," said her mother. "You don't have your helmet on. And it's hot out, so you need to fill up your water bottle."

Keisha groaned, but she filled the water bottle and strapped on her helmet. Soon, they were riding through the park on a bike trail. The sun was hot on her back, and Keisha was glad to stop for a drink from the bottle. When they got home, Keisha was tired but happy.

She couldn't wait for her next day off to go bike riding again.

Riding your bicycle alone or with friends can be lots of fun. It can help you get places you want to be, all on your own! And a bike doesn't use gas the way a car

Riding your bike is fun, but it is good to know some important safety rules.

does, so it's good for the environment. But even something as simple as riding your bike may lead to **accidents** that can hurt you or others. Before you hop on your bike, learn some safety rules so you can enjoy the ride.

CHAPTER TWO

How Do You Ride Safely?

There are a number of things to remember about bike safety. The first is to choose a good route. It is best to stay on streets and paths that you are familiar with. Don't ride against traffic. Instead, always ride in the same direction as cars are traveling. This means riding on the right-hand side of the street. Of course, if you are on a street that has bike lanes, use them!

When biking, be sure to watch and listen. Pay attention to the cars and people around

If you are trying to choose a safe biking route, bike lanes are usually a good idea.

you. You should never wear headphones when you are riding. You need to be able to hear everything that is happening. When leaving your driveway or an alley, always stop and check for traffic in both directions. And

You need to check for traffic before crossing a street with your bike.

look out for cars and other vehicles that are exiting driveways. They should watch for you, too, but they might not see you. Remember to stop and check for traffic at each corner. Also, try not to ride too close to parked cars. People get out of cars without warning, and a quickly opened door can be a danger to you!

As a bike rider, you should follow all the rules of the road, just as if you were driving a car. Ask an adult to review these rules with you.

Stop at all stop signs and red lights. At busy **intersections,** get off

your bike and walk it across the street. If you must pass another rider,

do so on the left—never on the right.

Bicycles don't have brake lights and turn **signals** like cars do.

But there are hand signals for turning and stopping that you should

learn. Here is a brief description. For a left turn, hold your left arm

straight out. For a right turn, hold out your left arm and bend your

If you're crossing a busy intersection, you should walk your bike across the street.

elbow up so that your arm forms an L. Always check for cars and

people behind you and in front of you before making turns. Before

stopping, hold out your left arm and turn it downward in the shape

of an upside-down L.

When riding your bicycle, never ride out into a street without

first stopping and looking both ways. Check behind you before

turning, swerving, or changing lanes. And

never follow another rider who is

not following these rules!

Riding with friends

can be great. But on

streets, be sure to ride in

single file. Riding side by side is

dangerous for you and

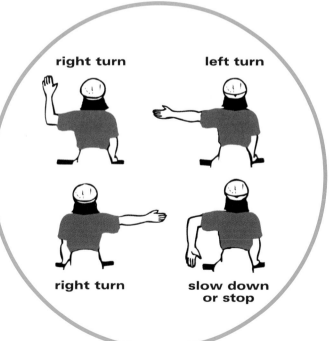

This diagram shows the proper hand signals for left and right turns as well as slowing down and stopping.

Lance Armstrong

Lance Armstrong is a champion cyclist. In 1995 and 1996, he won the Tour DuPont. This was a well-known race in the United States that lasted 12 days and covered more than one thousand miles (1,609 kilometers). However, soon after his second victory, Armstrong found out he had cancer, an often life-threatening illness. But he fought the disease. He went on to win the famous Tour de France four times in a row. That race is even longer than the Tour DuPont—over 2,000 miles (3,219 km).

You can bet that Armstrong knows how to stay safe on his bike. He always wears his helmet and keeps his bike in good condition. He remembers to drink plenty of water. And he always follows the rules of the road. In his races, Armstrong rides really fast. But, as most racers will tell you, being safe is more important than winning.

for other people using the street. And always ride with only one person per bike. Having someone try to balance on your handlebars or behind you is very dangerous. You can't steer or stop the bike properly with that extra weight. You could easily fall, and both of you could get hurt. If you ride safely, everyone can have fun.

CHAPTER THREE

WHAT DANGERS ARE THERE?

Roads can hold dangers for both cars and bikes. That's why it is important to watch the road ahead of you. Bumps in the road, potholes, and *grates* can cause you to lose control of your bike. It's best to travel across them slowly or to avoid them

Move slowly if you are forced to ride your bike across a grate, and always make sure to keep an eye on the road ahead of you.

Be sure to take your time if the road is bumpy or slippery!

altogether. Gravel and rocks can feel very different from a smooth surface. Slow down and take your time if the surface you are riding on suddenly changes.

Be especially careful if you are riding in bad weather. Remember that your brakes do not work as well when it rains. Ride more slowly and give your-self more time to brake. A quick stop can cause you to slide or fall.

Try not to ride on wet, slippery leaves, either.

One way to bike safely is to be predictable. This means that you should not do things that drivers or other bikers do not expect. Don't swerve or stop suddenly. Being aware of your surroundings will help you be predictable while riding your bike. You will be able to slow down when you see a dog run into the road ahead of you instead of stopping sharply. If you see a large pothole coming up, you will be able to signal that you are moving into another lane instead of swerving suddenly into traffic.

Always listen for shouts, sirens, and other loud noises. A

Always be aware of your surroundings so you don't have to stop sharply if a dog runs into the road ahead of you.

shout could mean that there is a problem or an accident. A siren could mean a police car, a fire engine, or an ambulance needs to hurry along. Pull over and stop to let these vehicles pass. Other noises could be a child running into the street to chase a ball. Be aware of anything entering the path in front of you.

You need to be careful of strangers while you are riding, just like you do on the playground or at home. If anyone you do not know

If you are on your bike and hear an ambulance coming, pull over and let it pass you.

Never forget to lock up your bike when you are done riding.

offers you a ride, say no and keep riding. If the person keeps asking or follows you, shout and make lots of noise. Look for a police officer or another adult you can trust, such as a neighbor or store owner.

When you get off your bike, always lock it up. The best place to lock your bike is in a bike rack, if one is available. Sometimes you will need to lock your bike to a fence or to a tree. Whether you stop at a store, at school, at someone's house, or at a park, always be sure your bike is secure before you leave it.

CHAPTER FOUR

WHERE ARE THE BEST PLACES TO RIDE?

There are many places to ride, depending on where you live. You can ride on streets in your neighborhood in the city or on dirt roads if you live in the country. You can also ride on bike paths that have been created in parks and along the sides of busy roads.

Riding on a flat, smooth surface is the best idea. If you do ride on hills, be sure to go down slowly. It is easy to go too fast and lose control of your bike when riding down a hill.

Perhaps you ride your bike on the streets in your neighborhood. Just make sure to always ride on a flat, smooth surface.

The sidewalk can be a safe place to ride as long as you respect other people using it. In some areas, it is against the law to skate or to ride a bike or scooter on sidewalks. Find out about the rules in your neighborhood. If you cannot ride on the sidewalk, try to avoid riding on very busy streets. Watching out for lots of cars can be difficult.

Each neighborhood has different rules. Find out in advance if it is all right to ride your bike on the sidewalk.

Try to stay on streets where people know you. It is nice to think that others will be looking out for you, just as you look out for them.

Try to ride in areas where you know people.

CHAPTER FIVE

WHAT SHOULD YOU WEAR
WHILE RIDING A BIKE?

The most important thing to wear when you are riding is a

helmet. A helmet will protect your head if you should fall or have

an accident. Make sure your helmet meets the safety standards set

by the Consumer Product Safety Commission (CPSC). A sticker

from the CPSC is on all

helmets that this agency

has approved.

Your helmet won't

help you if you are not

wearing it properly. Be

sure to wear your helmet

flat on your head, never

Always wear a helmet when you are riding your bike.

tilted forward or backward. Your helmet should have strong, wide straps. Fasten them snugly under your chin and keep them fast-

Make sure your helmet has strong straps and fits snugly.

ened while you are riding. Your helmet should fit well enough that it cannot move around on your head. Most helmets come with padding to ensure that you have a tight fit. The padding can be adjusted or removed as your head grows.

Your helmet is a tough piece of equipment, and it

Wearing bright colors (above) when you ride your bike will make it easier for people to see you. Dark colors (right) make it more difficult.

can save your life. You will need to

get a new one every five years. If you

have a hard fall and your helmet is damaged, replace it immediately.

The clothes you wear while riding are important, too. Fluore-

scent or bright-colored clothing makes it easier for other people to

Wearing riding gloves will protect your hands.

see you. Stay away from dark clothes, such as navy, brown, or black. If

you are riding in warm weather, wear lightweight clothing so you do

not get too hot. In cold weather, be sure to bundle up in a jacket and

earmuffs. In any kind of weather, riding gloves can protect your hands.

Try not to wear pants with wide legs. Loose material can get tangled up in your bike's chain. You can tuck your pants into your socks while riding to avoid this problem. You can also buy pants clips to keep the cuffs of your pants from getting in the way. Wear shoes that grip the pedals well. Try not to wear cleats, open-back shoes, or shoes with heels. And never ride barefoot!

The shoes you wear should grip the pedals of your bike well.

CHAPTER SIX

WHAT SHOULD YOU CHECK ON YOUR BICYCLE?

Before riding, you should make sure that your bicycle is in good condition for biking safely. Check the bike's owner's manual for safety advice. In addition, you can follow these tips.

Make sure your bike is the right size for you. Stand with one leg on each side of your bike and with your feet flat on the

This bicycle is too big for either of these girls.

ground. There should be

an inch or two

between you and the

top bar of your bike.

Then try sitting on

your bike with one foot

on the pedal and one foot on

the ground. Your foot should

It's a good idea to tighten your bike's wheels before going for a ride.

easily reach the ground, and the knee of your other leg should be

slightly bent. If this isn't the case, you need to change the height

of your seat.

Before riding, tighten your bike's seat, wheels, and handlebars.

Double-check that your wheels are straight. Check your brakes to

make sure they do not stick. Inspect your tires to see if they have

The reflectors on this girl's bike will help people see her if she rides in the dark.

the right amount of air. Oil your chain regularly, and check that it is moving smoothly.

Putting **reflectors** on your bike is a great idea. Reflectors help other people see you, especially if you are riding when it is almost dark. You can put reflectors on your wheels, behind your seat, on your pedals, and on your handlebars. Reflectors are a must if you are riding at night, though only older, experienced riders should be out after dark. Riding at night can be dangerous, since it is hard for others to see you.

Even if you don't often ride at night, a headlight is a good addition to your bike. It helps you see and helps others see you. Also make sure you have a bell or horn that works. Blowing your horn or ringing your bell tells others that you are coming or warns them of danger.

If you have to carry anything while you ride, attach a basket to your handlebars or a rack over your rear tire. Carrying a backpack can throw you off balance, so if you must carry one it should be light. Also, make sure the straps of your backpack are not too long. They might get caught in the wheels or the chain.

Before you ride, take the time to think about where you are going. Check your bike and review what you are wearing. Following these safety rules will make your bike ride a better one!

Glossary

accidents (AK-si-duhntz) Accidents are events that take place unexpectedly and often involve people being injured.

alley (AL-ee) An alley is a narrow passageway between backyards, homes, or other buildings.

grates (GRAYTES) Grates are groups of metal bars that are sometimes located in a street. These grates provide a place for water to drain during a storm.

intersections (in-tur-SEK-shuhnz) Intersections are the points where two or more streets meet.

owner's manual (OHN-urz MAN-yoo-uhl) An owner's manual is a book of instructions for a given item or piece of equipment.

reflectors (ri-FLEK-turz) Reflectors are shiny items that bounce back light that is shined on them.

route (ROOT) A route is a path or course that you follow from one place to another.

signals (SIG-nuhlz) Cars have turn signals, which are blinkers that warn other drivers about right and left turns.

Questions and Answers about Bicycle Safety

What if my friends say that riding with a helmet isn't cool? Tell them that getting hurt is not cool and that using a helmet helps prevent head injuries. Show them how you can decorate your helmet to fit with your style!

How should I ride on a road with traffic going two ways? Always ride on the right-hand side and follow the flow of traffic.

How should a friend ride with me on my bike? He shouldn't! One passenger per bike is the only safe way to ride, unless the bicycle is built for two.

What should I do if I am riding in really hot weather? Dress in lightweight clothing, carry plenty of water to drink, and stop to rest if you get too tired.

Helping a Friend Ride Safely

▸ Offer to ride with your friend so you both can remember the safety rules.

▸ Go with your friend to pick out a helmet that fits and meets safety standards.

▸ Friends should help each other check their bikes before riding.

▸ Suggest a route that you both are familiar with, using roads that have bike lanes or that do not have heavy car traffic.

Did You Know?

▸ More than 70 percent of bike accidents occur at driveways or intersections. Watch out for cars at both places!

▸ Most people who are hurt in bike accidents suffer from head injuries. Helmets can help prevent such injuries.

▸ Helmet standards were upgraded in 1999. Be sure your helmet is up-to-date.

▸ You should keep both hands on your handlebars, except when making hand signals to turn or stop.

How to Learn More about Bicycle Safety

At the Library

Bundey, Nikki. *On a Bike.* Minneapolis: Carolrhoda Books, 1998.

Carter, Kyle. *On Bicycles.* Vero Beach, Fla.: Rourke Publishing LLC, 1994.

Hayhurst, Chris. *Bike Trekking: Have Fun, Be Smart.* New York: Rosen Publishing Group, 2000.

Wood, Tim. *Road Travel.* New York: Thomson Learning, 1993.

On the Web

Visit our home page for lots of links about bicycle safety:
http://www.childsworld.com/links.html

Note to Parents, Teachers, and Librarians: We routinely verify our Web links to make sure they're safe, active sites—so encourage your readers to check them out!

Through the Mail or by Phone

National Center for Bicycling and Walking
1506 21st Street, N.W.
Suite 200
Washington, DC 20036
202/463-6622

National Center for Injury Prevention and Control
4770 Buford Highway, N.E.
Atlanta, GA 30341
770/488-1506

National SAFE KIDS Campaign
1301 Pennsylvania Avenue, N.W.
Suite 100
Washington, DC 20004
202/662-0600

National Safety Council
1121 Spring Lake Drive
Itasca, IL 60143
630/285-1121

The Nemours Center for Children's Health Media
Alfred I. du Pont Hospital for Children
1600 Rockland Road
Wilmington, DE 19803
302/651-4046

U.S. Consumer Product Safety Commission
Washington, DC 20207
800/638-2772

Learning bicycle safety early in life will lead to years of safe riding and exercise.

Index

About the Author

Lucia Raatma received her bachelor's degree in English literature from the University of South Carolina and her master's degree in cinema studies from New York University. She has written a wide range of books for young people. When she is not researching or writing, she enjoys going to movies, practicing yoga, and spending time with her husband, their daughter, and their golden retriever. She lives in New York.